Our God-Given Senses

Our God-Given Senses

**An introduction to the nine human senses
integrated with a study of the Bible**

by Gary A. Burlingame

Healthy Life Press
Orlando, Florida

OUR GOD-GIVEN SENSES

©2013 by Gary A. Burlingame
All Rights Reserved.

Published by:

Healthy Life Press • 2603 Drake Drive • Orlando, FL 32810
www.healthylifepress.com

Cover & Internal Designs: Judy Johnson

Printed in the United States of America

No part of this publication may be reproduced, stored in a retrieval system, or transmitted in any form or by any means—for example, electronic, photocopy, recording—without the prior written permission of the author, except for brief quotations in printed reviews.

Library of Congress Cataloging-in-Publication Data
Burlingame, Gary A.
  Our God-Given Senses

ISBN 978-1-939267-73-3
1. Reference; 2. Human Senses; 3. Bible Study

Undesignated Scripture references are taken from THE HOLY BIBLE, NEW INTERNATIONAL VERSION®, Copyright© 1973, 1978, 1984 by the International Bible Society. Scriptures marked KJV are from the King James Version of the Bible. Scriptures marked NASB are from the New American Standard Bible, Copyright© 1960, 1962, 1963, 1968, 1971, 1972, 1973, 1975, 1977 by the Lockman Foundation. Used by permission. All rights reserved worldwide.

Most Healthy Life Press resources are available in printed or electronic forms worldwide through bookstores and online outlets, depending on their format. This book is for sale in printed form or in a downloadable and printable eBook PDF format from *www.healthylifepress.com*. Commercial eBooks for all readers are available via: *eChristian.com*; for "Kindle" at *Amazon.com*; for "Nook" at *BN.com*. Retail sales are primarily through Amazon.com. Redistribution of printed or eBook formatted copies, regardless of their source, without written authorization violates international copyright law, and is strictly forbidden.

Preface

As a scientist, for more than twenty-five years I have used the human senses to solve environmental problems. In this book I review a small part of the vast scientific and medical information that exists today. As a Christian, I have studied God's Word for what he has revealed to us for spreading the aroma of life which is the knowledge of Christ. The two disciplines came together for me in this book as a Bible study version of *Richer Descriptions: A Guide to the Human Senses for Christian Speakers and Writers*. It was a joy for me to write this book, and I hope it brings you joy as you come to a better appreciation of the wonder of your God-given human senses (Psalm 139: 13-14).

Contents

Chapter 1	Created for a Sensory Experience	11
Chapter 2	Taste that the Lord is Good	15
Chapter 3	Breath of Life	23
Chapter 4	A Sense of Discernment	27
Chapter 5	A Pleasing Aroma	31
Chapter 6	The Smell of Sin	37
Chapter 7	The Anointed One	41
Chapter 8	Fishers of Men	47
Chapter 9	Faith Comes by Hearing	53
Chapter 10	Stand and Walk in the Lord	57
Chapter 11	A Healing Touch	61
Chapter 12	Tremble Before God	65
Chapter 13	Seeing is Believing	69
Chapter 14	The Appearance of Christ	73
Afterword		79
For More Information		81

Our God-Given Senses

Chapter 1

Created for a Sensory Experience

Our senses are a gift from God (Exodus 4:11). Thus, the Bible refers directly to taste, smell, touch, vision, and hearing. Faith comes by hearing (Romans 10:17). The name Ishmael means "God hears" (Genesis 16:15). Jesus touched the sick to heal them (Matthew 14:35-36; Mark 8:22-25). Our God is a God who sees (Genesis 6:11). The Word is a light unto our path and Jesus is the light of the world (Matthew 5:14; 1 John 1:5-7). The idols of wood and stone could not speak, see, hear, smell, feel, or touch (Psalm 115: 4-7), but the God that we know has always watched and listened to His people, smelling their sweet sacrifices and walking among them. When Jesus appeared to His disciples after rising from the dead they thought He was a ghost, but He told them to touch Him, see Him, hear Him, and behold His appearance (Luke 24:37-40).

To sense is to perceive. Something that is sensual is something that is perceived by the senses. While we have five that are well-recognized (taste, smell, vision, hearing, and touch), our sensory perception involves more than just our eyes, ears, nose, mouth, and fingers. Scientists and medical experts today define nine senses, not just five. These include the senses of pain, temperature, joint and muscle position, and gravity.

Our kinesthetic sense relies on receptors and neurons in our muscles and mobile joints such as our knees, elbows, and shoulders. These receptors detect the body's position and movement as with the positioning of our arms to judge weight because it takes body position and muscles to hold something up against gravity. The kinesthetic sense is highly trained by gymnasts, skaters, ballet dancers, and weight lifters. Did you ever wonder how a baseball player can run deep into left field to catch a fly ball? His senses keep him in balance, help him judge his movement and speed, and provide him with the ability to raise his glove at just the right time and place to catch the ball.

Proprioception, or body awareness, is an integration of the kinesthetic sense (of body movement) with equilibrioception (the vestibular sense) which allows us to accomplish complicated tasks such as walking with our eyes closed while reaching for a doorknob. A proprioception dysfunction makes us clumsy, uncoordinated, and accident-prone.

Exteroception (such as sight and hearing) keeps us in touch with our environment, whereas interoception (the cutaneous, kinesthetic, vestibular senses) keep us in touch with our bodies. The somatosensory system (*soma* means body) includes the cutaneous sense (body temperature, pain, visceral sensations, inflammation, itching) which uses receptors in the skin to provide the senses of touch, pain and temperature.

We learn by using our senses, but how we learn differs from person to person. Some of us learn by listening (we are auditory learners) or seeing (visual learners). Some need to touch (are tactile) or do something (kinesthetic) to make experiences take root. And we typically learn by using a combination rather than relying on any one sense.

> Scientists and medical experts today define nine senses: taste, smell, touch, vision, hearing, hot and cold, pain, balance, and body movement.

Our senses are distorted, even at times dysfunctional. Smell is subject to anosmia, cacosmia, dysosmia, heterosmia, hyposmia, parosmia, phantosmia, and even synesthesia. Though our senses are interlinked in amazing ways, synesthesia is a condition where they overlap—for example, where a person hears sound but envisions a color or shape or pattern. Colored hearing is the most common form of this disorder. Adaptation occurs when continuous stimulation results in a loss of awareness or in the detection of changes that stimulate our receptors. For example, we might adapt to a hat on our head and forget it's there.

In a spiritual context, through sin we lose our ability to hear properly and exercise discernment, and as a result we lose God's blessings (Deuteronomy 4:32-33; Isaiah 6:8-10; Amos 8:11-12). Our senses weaken with age; hearing and vision tend to decrease with age more quickly than smell. Disease and injuries as well as certain medications affect us such that a loss in one sense might predict the onset of a disease. For example, a loss in smell can be one predictor of Alzheimer's Disease or it can bring about poor eating habits, weight loss, and poor nutrition which in turn may lead to depression.

As a baby comes into the world she experiences a sensory wonderland. Her hearing is at its finest. She develops odor recognition of her mother and her taste buds are hyper-sensitive to sweet. Since her mother's diet affected the amniotic fluid, she acquired taste preferences before she was born. Now her mother's milk continues to expose her to her mother's diet as the milk carries the flavor of the food her mother eats. And her rapid growth requires healthy exposure to touch, hearing, smell, and sight. In comparison to a baby, God also calls us to use our senses to grow and mature and become more like Christ.

Bible Study Verses

Genesis 6:11	Luke 14:12-24
Psalm 34:8	Romans 10:17
Isaiah 6:8-10	1 Corinthians 12:14-26
Amos 8:11-12	James 1:22-25
Matthew 5:14	1 John 1:5-7
Matthew 14:35-36	Revelation 3:15-16
Mark 8:22-25	

Chapter 2

Taste that the Lord is Good

There is more to the experience of eating food than just the sense of taste. The whole of the experience is described as flavor. Flavor involves the olfactory sense (smell) and the gustatory sense (taste) as well as thermal (hot, cold), pain, and texture (mouth and nose feel) sensations. Our nose, mouth, and associated passageways are lined with nerve endings that provide sensations such as spicy, slick, drying, and astringent.

"Taste" is a very general term that can mean to test, set to trial, inspect by touch, as well as to observe the flavor. Scientifically, however, taste refers to sweet, salty, sour, and bitter sensations from the taste buds in the mouth, most of which are found on the tongue. Some people are "super-tasters"—they have a higher density of taste buds on their tongue which gives them a heightened sensitivity to bitter. Sweet can come from sucrose or sugar. Salty can come from table salt or sodium chloride. Citric acid, as found in lemon juice, is sour. Caffeine is bitter. Whereas sweet tastes are related to good things, such as milk and candy, bitter is associated with bad things such as poison. Yet bitter is critical in the flavor of many of our favorite foods (such as chocolate) and beverages (such as coffee and beer). Caffeine's lingering bitter taste provides added benefits by helping to balance the overall flavor of various beverages.

There is a fifth taste, known as "umami" (or savory). It is a Japanese term and comes from the meaty, protein-like sensation enhanced by the use of monosodium glutamate (MSG). Umami can be found in fish sauces, mushrooms, some cheeses, soy sauce, cured meats, and broths.

The Word of God and wise loving counsel are sweet like honey (Psalm 119:103; Proverbs 16:24 and 24:13). Honey contains sugar such as fructose and glucose. Fructose is the sweetest of the sugars. Babies have sweet taste buds all over their mouths, giving them an intense desire for their mothers' milk (which is full of fat and sugar, or nutrients and calories) while reducing stress, crying, and metabolic rate to allow the calories to fuel their rapid growth and development. As a child is trained to eat honey for his health, so we should train our children to enjoy the Word of God.

Sweet causes a desire for more, and chocolate plays on this desire (we have a "sweet tooth" for candy). The bitterness of medicine can be masked by the sweetness of sugar. A sweet taste encourages us to feed on energy-rich carbohydrates which in turn induce our body's release of chemicals that produce a feeling of calmness. Thus, when something is said to be sweet, it has a good and desirable quality.

Bible Study Verses

Exodus 15:25	Proverbs 24:13
Nehemiah 8:10	Song of Solomon 5:13
Psalm 19:10	Song of Solomon 5:16
Psalm 119:103	Isaiah 43:24
Proverbs 9:17	Amos 9:13
Proverbs 16:24	Revelation 10:9-10

Genesis 27:34 lays a foundation for the Bible's reference to bitter. When Esau was spoken to by his father, he cried out with a bitter cry. Bitter relates to sorrow and judgment, and even to death (Deuteronomy 32:32-33). It is part of the symbolism in Passover, the Jewish tradition that commemorates their freedom from Egypt. The Seder, on the first day of Passover, includes ground bitter herbs (such as horseradish) to represent the bitterness of slavery, to draw tears to the eyes. Grief, pain, and sorrow are often said, poetically, to leave a bitter taste. The historical context of Passover is the redemption of God's chosen people from their bitter bondage in Egypt, thus the eating of bitter herbs.

Gall is referred to in the Bible (Job 16:13; Matthew 27:34). Poisoned water is called water of gall in Jeremiah 8:14, 9:15 and 23:15. The word gall can be interchanged with the word bitterness (Job 17:13; Matthew 27:34; Acts 8:22-23). A bitter taste is associated with poison or bad things as with Moses and the Pharaoh; such waters were a curse from God. Roman soldiers offered Jesus a drink of wine vinegar. It might have contained gall or myrrh, making it bitter. It was offered on the stalk of the hyssop plant (Mark 15:23).

There are experiences in life that leave us with a bitter taste in our mouths. Naomi wanted to be called Mara because of the bitterness of her life (Ruth 1:20). In Romans 8:18-23 we find examples of the taste of sin: we have present sufferings; creation is subjected to frustration; sin's bondage leads to decay; we feel the pains of childbirth; and we groan inwardly.

Bible Study Verses

Exodus 12:8	Ecclesiastes 7:26
Exodus 15:23	Isaiah 5:20
Numbers 5:18	Isaiah 24:9
Numbers 5:23-24	Jeremiah 2:19
Deuteronomy 32:32	Acts 8:22-23
Job 3:20	Hebrews 12:15
Proverbs 5:3-4	Revelation 8:11
Proverbs 27:7	Revelation 10:9

Salt had a variety of uses. For example, it was applied to the wounds of the body in order to stop bleeding and halt infection, as well as to sting a punished person back to consciousness. The Bible makes little use of salt, yet what it does say about it is very profound. Genesis 19:26 is perhaps the most famous reference in the Old Testament where Lot's wife became a pillar of salt; a salt that was no longer good for any use.

> The Bible references all four of our common taste sensations: sweet, salty, sour, and bitter.

Matthew 5:13-16 tells us to be the salt of the earth, but a salt that remains useful (Mark 9:50). A mined form is pure, clear, and of high quality for food preservation and flavoring, and it is good to be consumed. Offerings to God were to contain salt (Leviticus 2:13; Numbers 18:19). The word "salt" shares its origin with the word "salary"; historically, salt was traded as a form of currency. This gives meaning to the phrase, "You're not worth your weight in salt." But a form of salt that is evaporated from the sea is riddled with impurities that diminish its use and value. A salt that has lost its purity was thrown away (Luke 14:34).

We are called in Matthew 5:13 to be salt of the earth—to bring forth flavor. We are called to redeem and transform the world; not to just prevent deterioration (as a preservative) but to bring out the good flavor (transform the culture and glorify God). We also judge the taste of food by comparing it to the saltiness of our saliva which is high in salt content. God's Word is like salt, bringing flavor to our lives and allowing us to make quality judgments about what we take into our spiritual bodies.

Salt induces thirst. Perhaps this is one reason why salty popcorn is given out at movie theatres and why taverns provide salted peanuts to munch on. The salt makes us thirsty, so we buy more to drink. We are to be the salt of the earth. We are to encourage the people around us to develop an unquenchable thirst for the Living Water.

Bible Study Verses

Leviticus 2:13	Mark 9:49-50
Numbers 18:19	Luke 14:34-35
2 Chronicles 13:5	Colossians 4:6
Matthew 5:13	James 3:11

Nurtured grapes have a greater content of sugar and so they taste sweet. The Promised Land had large, sweet grapes. Wild grapes taste sour. The Bible refers to eating sour grapes, which is the complaining of God's people (Jeremiah 31:29-30). The children who grew up during the years of captivity in the Old Testament became angry because they had to live with the repercussions of their forefathers' sins—they had to eat sour grapes. Jesus tasted sour wine on our behalf so that we might enjoy the finest of sweet wine through His atonement.

Bible Study Verses

Psalm 69:21 Ezekiel 18:1-4
Jeremiah 31:29-30 Matthew 27:48

The tongue, which is important for tasting foods as well as for speech, is the author of many sins and is sharp like a serpent. The Bible points out that the tongue can be a blessing or a curse (James 3:1-12). The tongue can drip with honey, stick to one's mouth, burn in agony, or praise the Lord.

Bible Study Verses

Judges 7:5 Song of Solomon 4:11
Job 6:30 Isaiah 50:4
Job 29:10 Lamentations 4:4
Psalm 10:7 Ezekiel 3:26
Psalm 34:13 Mark 7:33-35
Psalm 39:1 Luke 16:24
Psalm 137:6 Romans 14:11
Proverbs 6:16-17 Philippians 2:11
Proverbs 12:18 Revelation 16:10
Proverbs 15:2, 4

Chapter 3

Breath of Life

The Lord God made man from the earth and breathed the breath of life into him, through his nose. The Spirit is the breath of God, and it moves like a mighty wind. When God's spirit swirled and flowed through Adam's nasal passages, was Adam imprinted with the scent of God? What is the purpose for our sense of smell? Do we have the capability to discern the things that smell of God versus the things that smell of death? The Bible has given significance to the nose, the sensory organ that is used for smelling, and to the sense of smell.

An odor is a smell or scent or stink, whereas an aroma is a spicy or sweet odor, perhaps referring to spices which have historically been so important in the flavoring of foods. Aroma and odor, which are used interchangeably, are perceived in two ways. First, when we inhale or sniff directly through our nose we pull in air that ascends to our olfactory bulb to be smelled. The other way that we smell is by retronasal smell. When we chew, sip, slurp, and swallow food we release volatiles that travel up through a back passageway in our throat to our nose, allowing us to smell what we swallow. If you want to experience retronasal smell, try drinking a flavorful beverage with your nose pinched. The elimination of nasal air-flow prevents your olfactory bulb from sensing the odors. Then open your nose, close your mouth and breathe through your nose. You will experience a burst of smell as the volatiles from your mouth flow up to the olfactory center in your nose by way of your retronasal passage.

> God breathed the Spirit of life into Adam through his nose, the sensory organ used for smelling.

Some people can be "blind" to the smell of certain chemicals (they just can't smell them at all) or they might have a weakened sensitivity (they can smell them but only when they are at high concentrations). A loss of smell can happen from brain damage or from a virus that has infected the olfactory system. An anosmic person cannot smell odors. People who lose their sense of smell, however, may still sense chemicals because many chemicals (such as ammonia and vinegar) elicit feeling sensations or nose feel (burning, drying, stinging) that can still be detected. With parosmia the sense of smell is distorted; a pleasant odor is perceived to be sickening. Women who are pregnant tend to be hyperosmotic or hypersensitive to smell. Phantosmia is where the brain signals an odor that is not really there.

The sense of smell is powerful and closely linked to our emotions and memory. Thus, it influences our mood and emotional state as well as our mental awareness. We rely on our sense of smell more than we think – we are constantly sniffing and sending messages to our brain. It happens without thinking until a sensation triggers a warning of danger or a memory.

Our sense of smell decreases with age—this has been proven by scientific methods. The Bible described the loss of smell (2 Samuel 19:31-37) when eighty-year-old Barzillai the Gileadite came from Rogelim to cross the Jordan with the king. Barzillai lamented about his age, emphasizing that he had only a few years of life left and his sense of taste (or smell) was gone and his hearing had faded. As we age and approach death, our senses become weaker and we become less discerning and perhaps more accepting of things we would otherwise avoid.

Bible Study Verses

Genesis 2:7	Psalm 146:4
Genesis 7:22	Isaiah 2:22
Job 12:10	Ezekiel 37:1-14
Job 27:3	Lamentations 4:20
Job 34:4	

According to the Bible, the nose can be a feature of beauty and a source of life, or it can be an instrument of judgment. In Genesis 24:47 and Ezekiel 16:12 we find that the bride's nose draws much attention. In 2 Kings 19:28 we read that a man is made a slave when a ring is put through his nose. In Genesis 2:7, God gave the breath of life through Adam's nose. To breathe life into man through his nose brought attention to the fact that life is derived from God and God is central to it (Job 12:10). And in turn, to please God we must become a sweet smell to His nostrils or the center of His being. This sensory organ is used numerous times in the Bible to describe God's anger (2 Samuel 22:16; Job 4:9; Isaiah 65:5). Exodus 15:8 is one example: God gave five blasts out of it. In Nehemiah 9:17 and Psalm 103:8, we find God slow to anger or "long-nosed." In Proverbs it is said that if you strike a man, he will bleed from it (Proverbs 30:33).

Bible Study Verses

Exodus 15:8	Psalm 18:15
Numbers 11:18-20	Psalm 115:4-6
2 Samuel 22:9	Proverbs 30:33
2 Samuel 22:16	Song of Solomon 7:4
Job 27:3	Isaiah 65:5
Job 41:20	Ezekiel 8:17
Psalm 18:8	Amos 4:10

Chapter 4

A Sense of Discernment

The sense of smell throughout the Old and New Testaments can present a pleasing aroma, as of life, or a foul odor, as of death. In 2 Corinthians 2:14-17 it says that when we accept Jesus Christ as our Savior we acquire the "sweet savor of Christ." Four aspects to aroma are given: (1) the knowledge of Him; (2) the aroma of Christ; (3) the smell of death; (4) the fragrance of life. Sin is a vile odor and associated with the smell of death and decay (Judges 3:22-25; Exodus 5:21 and 7:18). In 1 Peter 2:2-3 it says that we are to taste that the Lord is gracious and experience Him firsthand (Hebrews 6:4-6). Revelation 3:16 is a warning to those who are "neither hot nor cold" (to those who are insipid or tasteless). As God draws us to Himself we respond to His influence over other influences—over Satan, the world, and our flesh.

In the story of Esau and Jacob (Genesis 27), Esau was a man of the field and the earth was his bed. His clothing smelled of plowed earth. Jacob was Rebekah's favorite and stayed home. Rebekah made Jacob smell like Esau to obtain his father's blessing by using Esau's clothing because his father used his sense of smell to discern the favored son from the other one.

> As we grow in the Lord we are to become more discerning—tasting, touching, seeing, hearing and smelling in a spiritual sense.

There is a fruit called "miracle fruit" that comes from a small tropical African tree. The fruit contains a glycoprotein that causes sour or bitter substances to taste sweet; it takes the unpalatable and makes it desirable. When we taste food to decide if we like it or not, we make a decision based on a reference. Nothing is neutral. The issue is the reference we use. As we grow in the Lord we are to train our tastes to recognize the bitter from the sweet. Thus we need to exercise our senses (Job 12:11) or we can become anosmic and undiscerning. Satan's desire is to confuse or deaden our sense of discernment (Isaiah 5:20).

Chocolate, really good chocolate, is a very careful blend of bitter and sweet tastes from cocoa and sugar. Dark baking chocolate is quite bitter. A high quality chocolate uses high quality cocoa beans, dairy butter, and quality cream. Think of Jesus and how bitter was His death. He wept blood and endured the cross. Yet how sweet was His victory. Such a perfect blend of bitter and sweet no earthly chocolate could ever produce!

Poisonous drink and food often tastes bitter (Jeremiah 9:15 and 23:15). Such a curse or judgment in Revelation is associated with wormwood (Revelation 8:10-11). Wormwood is a name for a shrubby plant that flowers during late summer and yields a bitter extract. It has a strong minty, spicy, and aromatic odor. People thought it had magical powers. It is considered poisonous enough to keep moths under control. It is associated with decay, judgment, and death. In Deuteronomy 29:18 we read that we should make sure there is no wormwood within our fellowship because it is a bitter poison.

Discernment is a skill that involves tasting, touching, seeing, hearing, and smelling. The application of our senses has always carried with it a call to be discerning between the things of this world and the things of God. We are encouraged to taste and see that the Lord is good (Psalm 34:8). We are called to flavor our words with spiritual truth. We are called to serve the Lord with passion and boldness. We are not to be part of our world by simply deferring its deterioration (Revelation 3:15-16). We are to redeem the world for Christ: to be salt—not just for preserving it but for bringing out the aroma of life, which is Christ.

Bible Study Verses

Exodus 16:31	Song of Solomon 2:3
Numbers 11:4-9	Jeremiah 48:11
1 Samuel 14:29	Matthew 16:28
1 Samuel 14:43	Matthew 27:34
2 Samuel 19:35	Luke 14:24
Job 6:6	John 8:52
Job 12:11	Colossians 2:20-21
Psalm 34:8	Hebrews 6:4-6
Psalm 119:103	1 Peter 2:2-3
Proverbs 24:13	

Chapter 5

A Pleasing Aroma

We are to give off the knowledge of Christ like a sweet aroma, pure and undefiled, as if we represent Christ in His triumph. He became our sacrifice—an offering on the altar, pleasing to God. As we give off the knowledge of Christ, it rises like a sweet aroma pleasing to God. Incense also symbolizes the prayers of intercession of Christ on our behalf (Romans 8:34; Hebrews 7:25). We are to be like censers (2 Corinthians 2:14) spreading the fragrance of the knowledge of Christ and the gospel, and offering continual prayer to our Father in Heaven.

Incense was burned in covered vessels or censers that were used to broadly disperse the fragrance from inside. The incense of the Old Testament temple was a mixture of spices (Exodus 30:34-35). The blending was critical. A very common ingredient was and still is frankincense.

It is mentioned throughout the Bible. "Frank" means free, or that it was inexpensive and readily available. It burns with a white flame, giving off a pleasant balsamic odor.

Incense is rich in symbolism. In 2 Chronicles 2:4, Solomon burned incense in the name of the Lord. Incense comes from aromatic substances such that when it is burned it releases a fragrant odor. It must be set on fire and burned. Fire is essential for releasing its pleasing aroma. Offerings that were burned released smoke into the air and their sparks ascended toward heaven. Fire is a symbol of purifying, as to come forth as pure gold or to go through trial by fire. Daniel 3 describes three men who were put into the fire. God did not put out the fire; He stepped into the fire to be with them. Perhaps we too must pass through fiery trials to release our sweetest fragrance.

Bible Study Verses

Genesis 27:26-27
Leviticus 6:15
Leviticus 8:21-29
Leviticus 17:6
Leviticus 26:31
Numbers 18:17
Psalm 45:8
Song of Solomon 1:12
Song of Solomon 2:13
Song of Solomon 4:10

Song of Solomon 7:8
Song of Solomon 7:13
Ezekiel 20:41
Daniel 3:27
Hosea 14:6
John 12:3
2 Corinthians 2:15-16
Ephesians 5:1-2
Philippians 4:18

In ancient Egypt, incense played a part in religious rites such as burial ceremonies. The Book of the Dead explains how Egyptians used prayers and the burning of incense to help the dead resist corruption from evil spirits in the darkness, and to pass into the life hereafter to unite with their gods. It was also burned to please the idols (Jeremiah 11:12) and at the burial of kings in the belief that the pleasing aroma ascended to the nostrils of the god(s) who would then accept the spirits of the dead kings (Jeremiah 34:5; 2 Chronicles 21:18-19).

In the Bible, the temple had an altar for the burning of incense (Exodus 37:25-29). In Ezra 6:9-10 the burning of incense made sure that prayers for the king and his family were acceptable to God. A similar practice can be found in Job 1:5. In Numbers 29:1-6 we read that these were offerings of pleasing aroma made to the Lord by fire, symbolic of continuous praise and prayer (Exodus 30:7-8; Malachi 1:11) such that the prayers of the saints were like incense (Psalm 141:2; Revelation 5:8 and 8:3-4). As Aaron offered this burning prayer for Israel, so the Lord prays for His people (John 17:9). As Aaron entered into the holy place to burn incense, Christ entered heaven and offered up appeasement to the Father for His people. As incense was offered as an intercession to the High Priest (Revelation 8: 3- 4), so we too are to offer up continual sacrifices pleasing to God (Hebrews 13:15-16).

In the Old Testament the burnt offering and the grain offering involved incense (Leviticus 2:1-3). Oil and frankincense accompanied the meat offering. This symbolically foreshadowed the offering of Christ, where Christ was sacrificed and then ascended to heaven to gain our acceptance to God. Sacrifices or offerings that are not pleasing to God have a displeasing smell (Ecclesiastes 10:1; Joel 2:20) whereas pleasing sacrifices have a fragrant smell (Exodus 29:18; Leviticus 1:9, 1:13, 1:17, 2:9, 3:5, 3:16 and 4:31). The bad smell of our sin drives God away, thus we need the sweet aroma of a sacrificial substitute to draw God back (Genesis 8:21).

> God's people are to spread around them the pleasing aroma of Christ, like incense from a censer.

However, the sin offering was different—it did not use oil or incense on it because it was a sin offering (Leviticus 5:11-13). In this practice the blood of the sacrificed animal was poured down the side of the altar, the animal was burned on the ground, and the odor was not a sweet aroma. Blood was sprinkled on the object before it was burned and the burnt offering was wholly burnt. Christ was a sin offering as His blood flowed down from the cross.

Incense and perfume were expensive and therefore kept in expensive alabaster jars that had tight seals to prevent evaporation and to keep out flies. This precious aromatic content was to be kept pure. We too are to keep the knowledge of Christ untainted, so that when we spread it to others it is pleasing to God. Yet while God fills us with the fragrance of Christ, which is the gospel, we are clay pots that crack and leak.

Certain types of wood, such as cedar and aloe, would be burned along with incense. Cedar has durable, aromatic and decay-resistant wood and thus it represented strength and lasting qualities (Hosea 14:5-6). An Egyptian embalming ritual involved rubbing the skin of the deceased with cedar oil and myrrh. The body would be stuffed with particles of aromatic cedar wood, and linen cloth would be used as a fragrantly perfumed body wrap to make the body pleasing for its afterlife. The Bible recorded the use of cedar wood (2 Samuel 7:1-2). The cedar of Lebanon is a large tree native to Lebanon and Turkey. It was used in the building of the temple. The tree's foliage gives off an aromatic odor when crushed and its fagots would be cast into the fire at the altar to add to the fragrance that was released.

Aloe is obtained from the core of a tree after it has been cut down. This wood has a soft, resinous quality and was desirable for perfumes. It was sometimes buried for a time to hasten its decay so that when it was burned it would give off a fuller aroma. There is a popular belief that the tree from which aloe perfume is obtained is the only tree descended from the Garden of Eden and is therefore called the Paradise Tree.

Bible Study Verses

Genesis 49:11	Psalm 45:7-8
Exodus 30:1	Psalm 133:1-2
Exodus 30:34-38	Psalm 141:2
Exodus 40:5	Song of Solomon 4:11
Leviticus 4:7	Ezekiel 8:11
Leviticus 10:1-2	Malachi 1:11
Numbers 16:46	Luke 1:8-11
2 Samuel 7:1-3	John 19:38-40
2 Chronicles 26:16-19	Revelation 8:3-4

Another way to fragrance the air for holy purposes was to scent clothing. Cassia was a popular spice of merchants (Ezekiel 27:19) produced from the beaten, powdered, and dried bark of a tree. Men used it to scent their garments. Aaron, as a high priest, had garments that smelled of myrrh and aloes in addition to the aroma of anointing oil (Exodus 29:21). Psalm 45:7-8 recorded a song of praise for the king wherein there was an anointing of robes with myrrh, aloes, and cassia. Those who follow in Christ's footsteps can be said to have upon them a fragrant covering (Psalm 45:7-8) such that when you bring these men together in unity you have a fragrant gathering (Psalm 133:1-2). Today, Jesus Christ is to be the perfume we pour upon our heads to fill our nostrils and to fragrance the air around us (Song of Solomon 1:2-4). In Genesis 49:11, clothes were washed in wine perhaps to foreshadow the Last Supper of Christ. Recall the burial of Jesus where Nicodemus brought a mixture of myrrh and aloes and wrapped Him up with the spices, in strips of fragrant linen, according to Jewish burial custom (John 19:38-40).

Chapter 6

The Smell of Sin

The fragrance of Christ is life to some but death to others. The following Bible verses explain this: "Now thanks be unto God, which always causeth us to triumph in Christ, and maketh manifest the savour of his knowledge by us in every place. For we are unto God a sweet savour of Christ, in them that are saved, and in them that perish: To the one we are the savour of death unto death; to the other the savour of life unto life" (2 Corinthians 2:14-16). The aroma of the knowledge of God can be a life-sustaining fragrance to those who accept Christ. But to those who do not, it is the aroma of judgment and death, for God uses the knowledge of Christ to convict.

In Daniel 3 we read about Shadrach, Meshach, and Abednego re-emerging from the very hot furnace of King Nebuchadnezzar. Their hair was not singed, nor their clothes charred, and they did not smell of smoke and fire. The Lord protected them with His holiness such that there was no sin to burn off or residual of sin to smell. Sin is associated with bad smells. In Jonah 4 we find that a worm got in the gourd of the vine and it withered. The sun beat down on the decaying gourd, which developed a vile odor such that Jonah became faint from the sun and the odor. To God, we are a stench unto death as we exist in an unsaved condition. We are a stench that is unbearable to be around.

The human body emits a great variety of chemicals that smell for a variety of reasons. Every one of us has a unique fingerprint of an odor profile-which a pet dog or cat can recognize-that is affected by age, sex, diet, genetics, health, use of medication, and the presence of disease. These human smells have assisted doctors in diagnosing disease. Our fingerprint odor profile changes over time from the pleasant smell of a young baby to the nauseating smell of disease in those who are dying. A body's odor will also change when exposed to fear, stress, and excitement. While normal perspiration is nearly odorless, body odors are produced by skin bacteria that decompose the fatty secretions from apocrine glands found in our armpits. Hair contains fats that absorb odors, thus, hairy people tend to be more odorous.

There are, generally, two types or classes of natural odors produced during decay: odors produced under aerobic or oxygen-rich conditions, and those produced under anaerobic or oxygen-deficient conditions. The smell of anaerobic decay is associated with death, while the smell of aerobic decay is associated with fermentation or moldiness. When a bottle of wine goes bad we don't say it died—we say it has gone moldy. When a road-kill stinks after being in the hot sun all day, we don't say the animal has gone moldy—we say it's a dead animal in the middle of the road. Anaerobic odors are the problem. They give rise to the stink of marshes, sewage, and infected pus.

> Every one of us has a unique fingerprint odor profile; in God's nose we were once the stench of sin but now we are a fragrant offering.

All living things are composed of proteins and amino acids such that, when they decay, microorganisms decompose their proteins and amino acids to make odors that smell like rotten eggs or dead fish. Two chemicals particularly stand out. Cadaverine, associated with the smell of human corpses, is very foul-smelling. However, you can buy cadaverine in a hunting supply store as an attractant for coyotes, fox, and other scavengers. It is even used to train search and rescue dogs. Putrescine is another obnoxious chemical similar to cadaverine in many ways. Both contribute to the smell of decaying flesh, but also make up the smell of bad breath.

The Bible, directly and indirectly, mentions unpleasant odors. Ecclesiastes 10:1 tells us that dead flies spoil a perfume and make it stink. As such impurities spoil a good perfume (Ecclesiastes 10:1), the Word of God is to be unmixed with worldly wisdom. Beelzebub was the lord of the flies for the Philistines—their land was infested with annoying flies. The Jews used this name to demean their god to be a god of dung or of the unclean. In Nehemiah 2:13 we read that one of the gates at Jerusalem was the dung gate or the place where the waste of the city was expelled. This was not the gate through which you would enter the city!

One thing is sure, that without Christ to save us we are all destined for a sensory nightmare. Ears will hear the weeping and the gnashing of teeth in Gehenna, Hell, Lake of Fire, or Lake of Burning Sulfur. The putrid smells of sulfur and burning flesh will be so strong that they will impart a bad taste in the mouth. The visual experience will be frightening and horrible. The skin, which is the largest sensory organ of the body, will overload the brain with pain (Revelation 16:10-11). Those trapped inside will be screaming and choking, having an uncontrollable shaking, a clawing out of the eyes, and a puncturing of the ear drums.

The message of Christ is salvation from this sensory hell. Martha warned Jesus to not remove the stone to Lazarus' tomb (John 11:38-40) because Lazarus had been dead long enough to begin to stink. The smell of the decaying body would have been sickening. But Jesus called Lazarus out to take off his rags of death and decay and to put on the fragrance of new life. The same is true for us; Christ experienced death (Hebrews 2:9) so that we could become a pleasing aroma to God.

Bible Study Verses

Proverbs 5:3-4	Amos 4:10
Lamentations 3:15	Amos 5:7
Lamentations 3:19	Revelation 8:10-11

Chapter 7

The Anointed One

The art of making perfume dates back to the Egyptians, who used natural fragrances and spices quite liberally for pleasure as well as for burial and religious occasions. The art of perfuming as described in the Old Testament was acquired during the nation of Israel's captivity in Egypt. In 1 Samuel 8:10-13 we read about daughters becoming perfumers, and kings taking these young women from their families for this purpose. By the time of Moses, priests had become the official perfumers.

Perfumes and spices were well used in the ancient civilizations of Egypt, Greece, Persia, and the Roman Empire. Everyday uses of perfume and oil offset body odors, provided skin care, prepared bodies for burial, and anointed honored guests. Egyptians used essential oils during massage treatments, a technique that today is called aromatherapy. The anointing of sick people was a medicinal technique done by rubbing scented oil into the body. Spices used in oils and perfumes included sandalwood, cardamom, myrrh, cinnamon, coriander, mint, and frankincense. They have been traded around the world, throughout history. The ingredients of perfume can also come from flowers such as geranium, rose, jasmine, orange flower, and ylang ylang. Today, synthetic products dissolved in alcohol have replaced the natural, more expensive fragrances. Such perfumes contain mixtures of chemicals that volatilize at different rates, creating a blend of scents that fade with distance and with time at different rates. A good fragrance properly applied creates tension, teases the nose, soothes the senses, invigorates the body, and arouses the emotions.

Proverbs 27:9 tells us that ointment and perfume can make the heart feel happy. In Isaiah 61:1-7 and Psalm 45:7 we read about the oil of gladness that penetrates deep into the heart and carries the fragrance of blessings. An ointment is a highly viscous substance used on skin as a cosmetic or salve. In the Bible the word ointment could be rendered anointing oil. God gave Moses instructions for making it that included a base of olive berry oil to which was added fine powders such as frankincense and myrrh.

Myrrh and frankincense are associated with the visit of the wise men to Jesus (Matthew 2:11) and both have symbolic meanings. Myrrh is mentioned many times throughout the Song of Solomon and in Genesis 37:25 we read that it was carried into Egypt because its gum was used in commerce, for healing and skin care, and to scent the garments of kings (Psalm 45:8). Its aroma is bitter, spicy, balsamic, and woody. The oil of myrrh represents our Savior, and we would use it to prepare the fragrance of the community of believers as the bride of Christ.

The Bible provides recipes for oils, ointments, and incense (Exodus 30:22-25) and the incense for the altar and the anointing oil used by priests had to be made in very specific ways (Exodus 30:31-33). Not only the equipment but the methodology had to follow God's strict standards. For example, perfumers were forbidden to crush spices under the wheel of a cart or to use a staff to beat cumin (Isaiah 28:27). A rod of just the right shape and weight had to be used to beat the raw materials into a powder. The oil base had to be from olives. The proportioning of ingredients had to be exact.

> The making of holy anointing oil used by the priests had to follow God's specific instructions in order to meet His high standards.

Pomade was a perfumed ointment used to groom the hair. The process for its preparation is called enfleurage, wherein a fragrance is transferred from flowers to an absorbent such as highly refined lard or tallow that was molded into slabs. Freshly picked flowers, with all impurities removed, were then placed between the slabs to allow their fragrances to be absorbed. Pomade de jasmin is made from jasmine flowers. An application of this is found in Esther 2:12-13, where women spent a full year in preparation for the day they would be presented to the king. Their bodies were treated as living pomades.

Holy anointing oil was the final product of the perfumer (Exodus 30:22-25 and 37:29). A priest, prophet, or king (Exodus 30:30) or an object (the temple) could be anointed with it (Exodus 30:25-29) to be consecrated and set aside for service to the king or to the Lord. Moses anointed the tabernacle and all its furnishings. Whereas in the Old Testament anointing was done with oil, in the New Testament we are anointed with the Holy Spirit and made righteous for service to the Lord, taking on the fragrance of Christ. The oil is one representation of the Holy Spirit (Psalm 89:20). In 1 Samuel 16:12-13, Samuel anointed David using the horn of oil and David became filled with the Spirit. In Acts 10:38, God anointed Jesus with the Holy Spirit because he is *The Anointed One*, the Christ.

The first mention in the Bible of using oil in this manner is in Genesis 28:18 when Jacob left his home, sand became his bed, and a stone became his pillow. He anointed the stone with oil of olives as an altar to the Lord. Olive oil was carried for minor injuries and for protection against the hot sun as well as for other purposes (Exodus 27:20), and in its pure form was an important part of the Hebrew diet (Numbers 11:7-8). There are over 200 references to it in the Bible. Neither animal nor fish oils, nor oils from the ground were acceptable. Proper oil was obtained from the best ripened olives, beaten and strained through finely woven baskets after which the product was decanted off the top of the remaining liquid. Gethsemane was the place where olives grew, were collected and pressed under heavy weight to bring out their valuable oil. Gethsemane is also where Jesus felt heavily pressed; where he sweated blood in prayer to our God, His Father.

Purified nard, or spikenard, was carried in an alabaster flask, vial, or jar. It comes from the root of an aromatic herb and was saved for special occasions. In Mark 14:3 we find a woman with an alabaster box. She broke the box and poured the ointment on the Lord as a sign that she acknowledged him as her Lord. In Matthew 26 Mary poured the liquid perfume or ointment on Jesus' head. In John 12, Jesus was anointed on His feet and then, not wasting any of the precious oil, the woman soaked up the rest with her hair. It was proper for a host to wash the feet of a special guest. Perhaps this was why Mark and Matthew focused on the unusual anointment of Jesus' head, as well as on the use of expensive, purified spikenard. Jesus commented that the perfume was good to use while He was yet alive (Matthew 26:12) since the custom was to save it for its owner's burial. Consider that Jesus went to His death still smelling of the aromatic oil or perfume that Mary had lavishly poured upon Him. It was not the religious officials who anointed Jesus, but a sinner out of humble sacrifice using a very expensive perfume that she had saved in an ornate alabaster jar for her own burial. Mary did not realize the symbolism of her actions for the life of Jesus. Perhaps, though, she did somewhat comprehend who He was and more importantly, the great thanks to be given Him after He raised Lazarus from the dead.

Bible Study Verses

Exodus 29:7	Proverbs 27:9
Exodus 29:21	Ecclesiastes 10:1
Exodus 30:22-29	Matthew 6:16-17
Exodus 40:9	Mark 6:13
Leviticus 16:32	Mark 14:3-8
Deuteronomy 28:40	Luke 7:44-47
1 Samuel 8:10-13	John 12:3
1 Samuel 16:13	Acts 10:38
2 Samuel 14:2	1 John 2:27
Psalm 45:7	

Chapter 8

Fishers of Men

Fish was an important food in Bible times. Jesus and His disciples enjoyed eating fish (Mark 6:41; Luke 24:41-42; John 21:7-14). God's people moaned about manna, desiring the taste of fish instead (Numbers 11:5). One of the gates to the City of David was called the Fish Gate (2 Chronicles 33:14; Nehemiah 12:39). Jesus used the image of catching fish to call His disciples to become fishers of men.

Fish develop their flavor from the water in which they live. The same fish grown in different waters—such as Atlantic salmon compared to Pacific salmon—acquire differences in flavor. Catfish, salmon, and trout can be grown in fish ponds or by aquaculture. Prior to harvesting the fish from a pond, the buyer will microwave fillets for tasting to inspect for "taints" or off flavors. Fresh fish brought in from the sea are kept on ice to deter their decomposition and are served as soon as possible (within a week) in order to provide the best flavor. We all know that dead fish can stink up a lake, or even the Nile as recorded in Exodus 7:21.

Fish is not the only food mentioned in the Bible. Fruit, nuts, wheat, bread and other foods can be found. In Judges 9:7-15 we find that a good king is like a vine, olive, or fig but a bad king is like a thorn bush. The good king gives up his life by being crushed as grapes or olives give up their sweetness when crushed, or by being broken open as with the fig. The good king is humble and sacrificial in his love, as exemplified by our king Jesus.

Spices, as mentioned in the Bible, can be any one of a number of aromatic natural products such as coriander which is a chief ingredient of curry powder and is mentioned in Exodus 16:31 with manna. The beneficial use of spice in food is associated with the enhancement of its flavor and its preservation. Spice plants contain powerful antibacterial and antifungal chemicals, provide macronutrients, improve the flavor of spoiled foods, and enhance human perspiration which increases body cooling. Cinnamon was of high demand and hard to get, but it was the delight of the kings. It was obtained from the bark and leaves of a tree that had been beaten into a fine powder. It has anti-bacterial properties and thus made a good spice for the preservation of foods.

The spice trade greatly affected the movement of peoples in the Holy Land. Ezekiel 27:17-22 tells us that an important part of the Old Testament economy consisted of its trading. Medical men and magicians used spices and herbs for cures and charms. Its value even brought warriors to the gates of Jerusalem (2 Kings 20:12-18). In Luke 11:42 we read that the Pharisees capitalized on the people's superstitions and practices, becoming wealthy in the use of spices.

A gift to Solomon from the Queen of Sheba was a gift of spices in abundance (1 Kings 10:10). King Solomon had a mountain of myrrh and a hill of frankincense (Song of Solomon 4:6) and many other fragrant materials that were grown in his gardens: fig trees (2:13); pomegranates (4:13 and 6:11); flowers (5:13) and beds of spices (6:2); apples or apricots (2:3); camphire and spikenard (1:14); cedar trees (1:17); mandrakes (7:13) and lilies (4:5); balsam trees oozing out myrrh (1:13) and all chief spices (4:14). Solomon described the very name of God as ointment poured forth such as with frankincense, myrrh, saffron, camphire, pomegranates, aloes, cinnamon, and calamus.

Bible Study Verses

1 Kings 10:10	Isaiah 39:2
1 Chronicles 9:29-30	Ezekiel 27:22
2 Chronicles 16:14	Mark 16:1
Song of Solomon 4:10	Luke 23:55-56
Song of Solomon 4:13-14	Luke 24:1
Song of Solomon 8:11	John 19:40

An Old Testament use of food was for feasts such as Passover and the feasts of unleavened bread and first fruits. They prepared God's people for the coming of the Master of the Banquet (Luke 14:12-24) who will one day provide a great wedding feast for His chosen people. Our words to one another, well-flavored, can be like save-the-date notices that engaged couples send out to friends and family—notices to not forget that a banquet is being prepared for God's people (Revelation 22:17).

> The collection of fish, breaking of bread, turning of water into wine, and use of spices remind us that God has prepared a feast for His people.

The feast of the New Testament is the Lord's Supper or Communion. The communion sacrament is a memorial to the birth, life, death, and resurrection of our Lord Jesus Christ. It is centered on the breaking of bread and the drinking of wine. The bread symbolizes His body or flesh as we share in His temptations, suffering, punishment, and condemnation. The wine symbolizes His blood as we share in His judgment, atonement, and death. We must consume and taste of His suffering and humanity to truly accept His grace and be filled with the joy that goes beyond suffering.

Consider how Christ used wine to symbolize His blood sacrifice (Mark 14: 22-25) and that Jesus turned the water into wine at the wedding feast of Cana. It is sweet and drinking it makes the heart glad. To make wine you must pluck the fruit from the vine and crush it to release its juice or the blood of the grape (as in Genesis 49:11). Then it is fermented and aged to maturity.

Wine is the fruit of the vine. Jesus has been described as the vine and we as the branches, producing fruit that bears the fragrance of Christ.

In John 6 we read that Jesus is the bread of life. Passover makes symbolic use of bread. Leaven, or the yeast used to make bread rise, is a symbol for sin in both the Old and New Testaments. There was no leaven used in sacrificial bread offerings just as Christ, the Lamb of God, had no sin. Since bread is made by crushing kernels of grain to make flour, so our hard outer shells must be broken and removed to make us fit for daily service. This is the work of the Spirit in our lives—to remove the leaven from our hearts, to break us for service, and to make us humble and holy servants of the Lord.

The communion table is a feast and a delight to the senses. It is not just a tease but a spiritual wonder. It calls on us to taste the bread, enjoy the aroma of the wine, hear God's Word preached, and see and touch one another. As we taste the bread and the wine, we taste the victory of Christ over sin and death. We will never experience death (Matthew 16:28; Hebrews 2:9) since it has lost its sting for those in Christ.

Bible Study Verses

Genesis 3:19	Amos 9:13-15
Exodus 12:14-20	Jonah 1:17
Exodus 23:14-17	Matthew 4:4, 19
Numbers 11:4-6	Matthew 6:16-18
Deuteronomy 7:12-17	Matthew 7:9-12
Psalm 104:14-15	Mark 14:22-25
Ecclesiastes 9:7	1 Corinthians 5:6-8

Chapter 9

Faith Comes by Hearing

God speaks (Psalm 29:4) and hears (2 Kings 19:16). His voice thunders and breaks cedar trees (Psalm 29:5). Adam and Eve heard Him walking in Eden and God heard them (Genesis 3:8-10). The Bible reinforces the importance of hearing, but with a spiritual aspect to hearing God's living Word.

Audition refers to our sense of hearing. The origin of the word is linked to a time when people settled accounts by an oral recitation or audit; to have a hearing was to have an audience. Worship is a time of hearing, a time for witness and maybe even an audit. We hear the voices of God's people singing praise, shouting for joy, giving testimonies, and weeping. We hear the Word preached and the declarations of faith by those who are saved.

In order to hear we must receive sound waves, organize sound bits, and interpret the information. It's an amazing system! The outer ear collects the waves that move through air like ripples on a lake. The eardrum in the middle ear is a membrane that collects the wave energy, transferring vibrations to the hammer, anvil, and stirrup bones for amplification before forwarding them to the cochlea. The cochlea in the inner ear is filled with fluid that picks up on the intensity and frequency of the vibrations. Hair cells in the cochlea collect and forward the information to the auditory nerve, which carries it to the brain for processing.

The three main components of sound that the ear distinguishes are frequency, loudness, and pitch. Since sound moves through the air in compression waves, frequency is the number of waves per second. Loudness is the amplitude of the waves. Pitch is the tonal quality. The fact that we have two ears helps us judge which direction sound is coming from because sound waves do not reach both ears at the same time unless we are facing the sound head on or it is coming from directly behind us. Try bending your ears toward the front of your face, with cupped hands over them in the direction of sound. Notice how this enhances the sound.

As we age our ear drums thicken, hair cells die off, and high frequency sounds become harder to pick up so that when someone is speaking too quickly, or there are echoes, or we are in a crowded room, we have trouble understanding what we are hearing. Continuous exposure to loud noise can raise our blood pressure and change our mood. At birth we have the greatest capacity to distinguish between sounds but over time this capacity decreases as we experience progressive damage to our delicate hearing system.

God spoke to His leaders (Exodus 19:19; Isaiah 5:9)

and helped them in turn speak the truth (Exodus 4:12). And the truth of God, which is the witness of His love for His people, spread from ear to ear (Psalm 44:1). The Spirit of God accomplishes God's plan of salvation through His Word in both written and spoken forms for there is a spiritual hearing or understanding we obtain by faith in Jesus (Matthew 11:15; Matthew 13:9). If we are born of God by faith, we will hear God speak and we will recognize His voice (John 5:25; John 8:47; John 10:3-5; 1 John 4:6; Revelation 3:20; Revelation 22:17).

> If we are born of God by faith, we will hear God speak and we will recognize His voice.

What type of voice would you expect God to have if He spoke to you? As with facial expressions and body language, voice qualities such as inflection, tremor, and diction play a role in how we respond to each other. Consider how important this is for a singer, actor, teacher, or pastor. A woman's voice tends to be higher pitched than a man's voice, and it changes with menstrual cycle, with puberty and with old age. An excited person would sound different than a very calm person at rest. We communicate not just by words but by changes in voice quality.

God does not promise to hear the voice of sinners who choose to turn away from Him (John 9:31). And if we are not born of God through faith but rather choose rebellion, or to live in sin, we will be deaf to Him or dull in hearing the truth (Psalm 38:13; Isaiah 43:8; Matthew 13:15; Acts 28:27). Yet there is hope. Jesus brought healing to those who were deaf or dull in hearing (Mark

7:33-37; Luke 7:22). Therefore, we must not refuse to hear God when He speaks to us (Hebrews 12:25).

Bible Study Verses

Genesis 3:10	John 3:8
2 Kings 18:12	John 9:31
2 Kings 19:16	John 10:3-5
Psalm 29:3-5	Acts 28:27
Psalm 38:13	Hebrews 12:25
Psalm 44:1	1 John 4:6
Matthew 13:9	

Chapter 10

Stand and Walk in the Lord

God used the example of a builder's plumb line to explain to Amos that the people of Israel were not upright. When we are not well-balanced, we do not walk straight nor stand upright before a holy God. Although God's requirements for Israel were unachievable, Christ achieved these on our behalf. Today, with God's Word, prayer and fellowship in the power of the Holy Spirit's presence, we maintain balance. We stand steadfast and straight when we put on the armor of God (Ephesians 6:10-18) against the spiritual forces of evil that constantly try to pull us off balance.

To be in equilibrium is to be in a well-balanced condition, having a healthy sense of balance or equilibrioception. Our inner ear consists of canals or chambers oriented at right angles to each other in three planes of rotation and filled with fluid. This alignment allows us to determine pitch (movement of the head in a "yes" manner), roll (tumbling left or right), and yaw (movement of the head in a "no" manner). The fluid shifts when our head moves, causing tiny hairs to detect it and alert our brain. When this action backfires, though, we experience motion sickness. With age the hairs die off and we become more unsteady with disequilibrium, even vertigo and nausea.

> Equilibrioception, our sense of balance, is maintained by the movement of fluid in our inner ear; wisdom and faith help us stand upright in God's presence.

Eustachian tubes connect the back of the nose to the middle ear, and open or pop to adjust pressure inside the middle ear behind the eardrum. Swallowing, yawning, or chewing gum activates muscles that help open the tubes. We feel as if our ears are blocked and sounds are muffled when the pressure on both sides of the eardrum is unequal. If blockage continues, fluid is drawn into the ear tubes which can lead to infections. Colds, sinus infections, and nasal allergies promote blockage by deterring the opening of the tubes and preventing drainage. Fluid filled ears affect our sense of balance.

Did you ever play the game of spinning around in a circle, stopping suddenly and trying to stand still? You stumbled and fell down. The fluid in your inner ear kept spinning even though you stopped. Your brain tried to compensate, but you lost balance. Our spiritual lives are like this at times. We spin in circles and get dizzy. But Christ calls us to stand firm and walk straight so as not to stumble or fall.

Bible Study Verses

Job 2:3	Matthew 15:14
Proverbs 4:12	Romans 11:11
Proverbs 28:18	1 Corinthians 10:12
Isaiah 28:7	Revelation 3:20

Chapter 11

A Healing Touch

The Bible speaks of God's hand or touch which can be mighty and convicting. The "finger of God" demonstrated His power to Pharaoh (Exodus 8:19), wrote out the Ten Commandments on stone (Exodus 31:18), and drove out demons (Luke 11:20). Using His finger, Jesus wrote a message on the ground that convicted those who had the eyes to see (John 8:6-8).

The skin is the body's largest sensory organ: it has receptors for touch (tactile sense), pressure, pain, and temperature. Sensory information is provided by nerve endings in the skin's surface and deeper tissue, hair follicles, sweat glands, and blood vessels. Hair follicles allow us to feel it when we brush our hair. Sensations also come from the bending and stretching of the skin's pores and nerve endings. The sense of touch exists internally throughout our body as in our throat, lungs, stomach, and intestines. Certain receptors are particularly sensitive to a gentle touch and these are abundant on our fingertips, lips, and tongue. They are also found on the palms of our hands and soles of our feet, as well as on our lips, eyelids, genitalia, and nipples. The receptors for the sense of pain are the greatest in number and women tend to have more of these than men.

Our skin, in communication with our brain, tries to keep our body temperature between 97° F to 99° F (36.5° to 37° C) avoiding hyperthermia and hypothermia. There are separate receptors for cold and hot because it is critical for the skin to adjust to changes in temperature. Cold receptors are most abundant on the tips of our nose, lips, and forehead. While sweat glands release body vapor and body heat to cool the body, your body will shiver to warm up when it's cold.

> Healthy human development, and the ability to love one another, involves the skin which is the body's largest sensory organ; it senses temperature, pain, and touch.

The sensations of cold and hot are described in the Bible. In a spiritual sense, God hates lukewarm people. He wants us to stand our ground and show whether we are hot or cold to His love (Revelation 3:15). If we are spiritually cold to God, and unrepentant of sin, God's breath will be icy upon us (Job 37:9-10), or His anger will burn against us (Judges 3:8), or His judgment will consume us like a fire (Revelation 16:8-9). Sin consumes us like a hot oven (Hosea 7:3-7).

Adam and Eve were forbidden to touch the fruit of a

tree in the Garden of Eden (Genesis 3:3). God continued to warn us that there are unclean things (Leviticus 7:21; Leviticus 11:8; Isaiah 52:11; 2 Corinthians 6:17) as well as holy things that we should not touch (Numbers 4:15; Psalm 105:15). But this sense can be deceiving. Anesthesia is the inability to feel the sense of touch and paresthesia produces sensations when nothing is happening. Tactile defensiveness is an over-reaction that can lead to fear, triggered by coming in contact with someone or something.

It is well known that the sense of touch is critical to the healthy growth of an infant. We need to be held by our parents. We need to experience one another by a hug, a holding of hands, a pat on the back, or a handshake. Normal emotional and physical growth requires a lot of touching. Touch has always been important for healing. A good doctor will use her senses to make a thorough physical examination of her patients, especially when diagnosing a medical problem. When Jesus walked the earth, people crowded around Him hoping to be healed by touching Him or His clothing (Matthew 9:20-21; Matthew 14:36; Mark 3:10; Mark 5:28; Luke 8:44).

When we kiss, we not only touch but we smell, hear, see, and sometimes taste the one we are kissing. It involves multiple senses in a very intimate way. Perhaps because of this, throughout history and in different cultures even today, kissing is not always something that is allowed to be done in public and or even at all. Nonetheless, God encouraged us to greet one another with a holy kiss (Romans 16:16; 2 Corinthians 13:12). We are called to kiss the Son and praise the Lord (Psalm 2:12). By contrast, Judas betrayed Jesus with a kiss (Matthew 26:48; Luke 22:47-48).

Bible Study Verses

Genesis 22:9-10

Exodus 8:19

Numbers 4:15

Matthew 9:21

Mark 5:28

Luke 11:20

Luke 22:69

John 3:35

John 8:6-8

John 10:28

John 20:25

2 Corinthians 6:17

Chapter 12

Tremble Before God

Moses trembled in fear of God. So did the demons. A person can tremble in excitement or in fear, because of actual pain or because of an expectation of pain, or because of old age.

A tremor is an involuntary, rhythmic oscillation of a body part or a muscle contraction. A barely noticeable tremor can become exaggerated under episodes of extreme cold or pain, stage freight, fatigue, stress, nervousness, or fever. It can also be drug-induced as with too much caffeine or lead or mercury poisoning. Diseases such as hypoglycemia, central nervous system disorders, thyroid disorders, stroke, and multiple sclerosis can bring about tremor. Psychological or psychiatric-associated forms are usually due to trauma, stress, and anxiety. One that lessens during movement but increases while resting is caused by Parkinson's Disease (PD), a neurologic disorder. Essential Tremor (ET) is a benign, hereditary form that is more noticeable during activity and increases with age.

> The sense of pain, which God can use for our good, is so complicated that science and medicine have not yet solved all of its mysteries.

One reason to shake or tremble is to respond to pain. Pain can be described as a sensory system in itself. It involves pressure, temperature, and chemical changes. It can result from changes internal to the body or from problems occurring on the skin. There are three different receptors or nerves for pain, ranging from an acute sharp pain to a dull lingering pain. It can be a chronic lasting ache. Chronic pain is believed to develop when the brain and spinal system of nerves establish a memory of a painful experience. There is first or fast pain that acts quickly and lasts as long as the nerves are stimulated. For example, when a finger is bent backwards we feel it. As soon as we stop bending it backwards, it stops. Then there is second or slow pain that lingers after the cause is removed.

Pain is an experience that arises from complex interactions involving memory, emotions, and the subconscious. It has many causes and includes subjective aspects that make it difficult to measure the level of pain from person to person. If pain is linked to a horrible memory or emotion, it can be heightened. Hyperalgesia is a disorder marked by an increased sensitivity to pain. Finally, a person who has lost a limb, as by amputation, can experience a Phantom Limb Sensation. This is where nerve endings and receptors continue to tell the brain that the limb is attached. This can also occur with a lost tooth. Pain is so complicated that science and medicine are still studying its many mysteries.

The Bible speaks of the introduction of pain into the world through sin. Judgment and sin bring forth pain and torment (Matthew 8:12; Matthew 25:30; Revelation 16:10-11; Revelation 20:10). Yet God has used pain to discipline or strengthen His people's faith (Job 33:19; Isaiah 13:8; Isaiah 26:17-18). Most importantly, we have the hope that the day will come when there will be no more pain (Revelation 21:4).

Bible Study Verses

Genesis 3:16-17	1 Corinthians 2:3
Genesis 27:33	2 Corinthians 7:13-15
Deuteronomy 2:25	Philippians 2:12
Ecclesiastes 12:1-3	Hebrews 12:21
Mark 16:8	James 2:19
Acts 16:29	

Chapter 13

Seeing is Believing

God has allowed us to see His work and blessings throughout history (Deuteronomy 3:21; 11:7). When the eyes of Adam and Eve were opened to good and evil (Genesis 3:5), sin came into the world. Blessings therefore bring about good vision while sin leads to blindness (Matthew 13:15-16; Mark 8:18). God favors those who follow in His ways (Genesis 6:8; 18:3; 19:19; 39:4; Psalm 34:15). God sees (2 Kings 19:16; Job 34:21-22) and does not miss the acts of the wicked (Genesis 38:7; 2 Kings 17:18). Therefore, we can plead to God to hear and see our prayers and praise, as well as to see and punish those who hate the Lord and His people (Isaiah 37:14-17).

The Word of God came at times in a vision (Genesis 15:1; 1 Samuel 3:1; Acts 16:9; 18:9; Revelation 9:17). To "see" is a way to seek the truth, to stay out of danger, to guide others, and to praise the Lord by the beauty of the creation which is His handiwork. Jesus appeared to His disciples in full sight after He arose from the dead (Luke 24:30-32). It was important that they saw Him with their eyes. It has always been God's plan that we lift up our eyes to Him with praise (Psalm 123:1-2). And one day there will be no more tears in our eyes (Revelation 21:4). Our eyes are well protected in several ways. They reside deep in eye sockets with eyelashes that protect against dirt and debris, and eyebrows that protect against sweat and water from our forehead. We blink to wet our eyes when the air is dry and for lubrication to counteract irritants such as dust, smoke, and allergens.

The mechanisms that produce our sense of vision are well understood. Our eyes detect color and light, and judge distance. The eye's retina consists of rods, or black and white receptors to detect shades of gray, and cones to detect color. The cones pick up the three primary colors of blue, green, and red. But to see color, our eyes need sufficient light. Thus at night we see shades of gray. When light is bright or intense, our pupils constrict. When light is weak or dim, our pupils dilate. Dilation can also occur when we are excited or feeling attracted to someone else. In the 1800s, some women took a drug called atropine or belladonna ("Beautiful Lady") to dilate their pupils to make them appear more attractive. Nocturnal animals are color-blind. Although color-blindness or color deficiency occurs in humans, it rarely limits a person to seeing only black and white. Common color blindness is the inability to see reds and greens; these colors appear as shades of blue and yellow.

We need two eyes to bring two slightly different images to the brain for image processing, to see peripherally, and to judge depth in three-dimensions. Optical illusions play off this interaction between the eyes and the brain. The brain tries to fill in what the eyes don't see. (The optical nerve is actually a part of our brain.) Artists have used this trick, too. They leave out details, letting the viewer's brain fill in the missing elements.

> It has always been God's plan that we lift up our eyes to Him with praise, and one day without any more tears.

Far-sighted people can see objects far off, but objects close by are fuzzy. Long-term damage from ultraviolet (UV) light can contribute to the far-sighted condition. Sunglasses with UV protection help protect the eyes. Near-sighted people can see close up objects, but objects far off are fuzzy. People who do a lot of close-up work with their eyes are more prone to becoming near-sighted. Whereas we go to eye doctors to have our vision checked and corrected, in the Bible it was Jesus who brought healing to the blind (Matthew 9:29-30; Luke 7:21; 18:42-43).

God created night and day, light and dark, morning and evening. He contrasted light and darkness to make spiritual truth come alive to us. Jesus is the light of the world, and we are to reflect that light like a lamp upon a table, which eradicates the darkness, bringing forth truth and hope. Light reveals what is unseen in darkness, bringing about repentance or judgment. While God gave His people the eyes to witness His work on earth, such as their freedom from Egypt and slavery, God still had to give us the eyes that see and ears that hear the spiritual truth that brings about salvation. And we are to keep our eyes open as watchmen ready to warn others of the dangers of sin (Ezekiel 33:6).

Bible Study Verses

Genesis 6:8	Job 34:21-22
Genesis 18:3	Psalm 34:15
Genesis 38:7	Ecclesiastes 11:7
Genesis 39:4	Isaiah 37:14-17
2 Kings 19:16	Matthew 7:3

Chapter 14

The Appearance of Christ

To meet someone face-to-face is to meet someone very personally and honestly. Jacob and Moses met God this way (Genesis 32:30; Exodus 33:11). As a result of meeting with God, Moses had to place a veil over his face as he walked among his people (Exodus 34:35). In the face of Christ we see the full glory of God (2 Corinthians 4:6) shining like the sun (Matthew 17:2). The face is a very complicated matrix of nerves and muscles that can produce more than forty different movements, which in turn create over 10,000 unique expressions. These movements help us protect our face, breathe, eat, talk, see, smell, and yawn. These movements help us communicate with each other.

Our face is determined at birth: the bone structure and arrangement of tissue; the eyes, nose, mouth and lips, chin and cheeks, forehead and ears. But changes occur as with wrinkles from age or with health problems such as caused by allergies, skin conditions, stroke and accidents. Nerve damage can cause a partial paralysis of one side of the face or it can reduce facial expressions in general, which can then interfere with relationships. This is because the face is critical in communication.

> God's design of a complicated matrix of nerves and muscles in the face helps us develop intimate relationships with each other through expression.

Facial muscles have been mapped to help experts better understand expressions which provide critical non-verbal communication and are linked to emotions. Expressions affect our social comfort as well as our feelings of security and success. They can be very slight such that we respond to them without realizing it, or they can be quite radical such as when we laugh, cry, or express horror. Some people are uncomfortable with looking into a person's face because they might over-react to facial expressions. Some people can hide emotional expressions (such as with a "poker face") or make up emotional expressions such as during play acting. These basic emotions have been categorized. One list gives six basic emotions: happiness, surprise, fear, sadness, anger, and disgust. Another list gives the following: amusement; anger; contempt; contentment; disgust; fear; guilt; embarrassment; excitement; pride in achievement; relief; sadness/distress; satisfaction; sensory pleasure; and, shame.

Indeed, to have God's face shine upon us is a blessing (Psalm 80:3, 7) while to have God hide His face from us is a curse (Psalm 27:8-9; Isaiah 64:7) as the face of the Lord is against those who willfully sin (1 Peter 3:12). Satan once challenged God that Job would curse Him to His face (Job 1:11; Job 2:5). An act of great respect and praise is to put one's face to the ground as an act of total submission and honor (Ruth 2:10; 1 Kings 1:23; Matthew 26:39). When Daniel interpreted King Nebuchadnezzar's dream, the king of Babylon fell on his face in great honor to Daniel and in humble recognition that Daniel's god was the God of all gods and King of all kings (Daniel 2:46). Someday we will see the face of our Lord in true intimacy, without any barriers or veil (1 Corinthians 13:12; Revelation 22:4).

Bible Study Verses

Genesis 32:30
Exodus 33:11
Psalm 27:8-9
Psalm 80:3, 7

1 Corinthians 13:12
2 Corinthians 4:6
Revelation 22:4

In the Bible, much could be determined by how a person dressed. Wealthy people or people of the king's household wore clothes of fine cloth of many colors especially purple, blue, and white (2 Samuel 13:18; Esther 8:15; Daniel 5:7, 16). God instructed men and women about their appearance to each other (Deuteronomy 22:5) and that clothing could carry disease (Leviticus 13:47). In Eden, Adam and Eve had enjoyed being naked (Genesis 2:25) until their eyes were opened in sin (Genesis 3:7). Then

God fashioned garments for them to wear (Genesis 3:21). In judgment and repentance, people tore their clothes and put on sackcloth to weep and wail and mourn (Genesis 37:34; 2 Kings 19:1; Psalm 69:10-11; Esther 4:1). Sackcloth was a coarse, dark colored cloth, perhaps of goat hair used to make sacks. It was worn without undergarments, close to the skin, during mourning and grieving.

God tells us that He does not judge us the same way we judge each other by physical appearance (1 Samuel 16:7; John 7:24). Appearances can be misleading as with a false prophet in sheep's clothing (Matthew 7:15). Yet the appearance of Jesus in all His glory is described as being in a white robe, shining with a face like the sun (Matthew 17:3; Mark 16:5; Acts 10:30-31). Coming is the day when God will clothe us in glory (Revelation 3:5). He will dress us in white and place on our heads a jeweled crown (Revelation 3:5, 4:4, and 19:14).

Bible Study Verses

Genesis 12:7	Daniel 10:18
Numbers 20:6	Matthew 1:20
Deuteronomy 31:15	Mark 16:9
2 Chronicles 7:12	Mark 16:14
Ecclesiastes 9:8	Luke 24:37-40
Daniel 8:15	

Afterword

Did the human sensory system come about after millions of years of evolutionary fine-tuning to give us a competitive edge for survival? Could this explain how physicians, today, train their senses to diagnose diseases, how athletes use their senses to win, and how mothers rely on their senses to protect their babies?

Perhaps the human senses are a channel between heaven and earth, between the spiritual and material. This could explain why alchemists used their senses to support their craft and why poets draw on sensory imagery to transport their audience to existential heights of awareness.

Or perhaps the human sensory system comes from an intelligent design. The handiwork of a Creator. A link back to Eden. A foretaste of the feast that awaits us. Even so, pastors and church teachers rarely talk about the human senses, and then only peripherally when their Bible studies touch on verses that coincidentally use sensory words.

God created us for a sensory experience. But why? To enjoy His creation? To make sure our bodies, as the temple of the Spirit, remain healthy? Perhaps. While God's truth is too deep for its full comprehension, He gives us glimpses of it, using tangible ways to help us understand. Since the Bible makes application of sensory words, and our nine senses are important for everyday life, then God may be teaching us eternal truths through sensory imagery.

Think on these things as you read Scripture, eat dinner, take communion, wear perfume, burn incense, anoint with oil, or simply smell the flowers.

For More Information

G.D. Armerding's *The Fragrance of the Lord: Toward a Deeper Appreciation of the Bible* (New York: Harper and Row Publishers, Inc., 1979) and D. Hocking and C. Hocking's *Romantic Lovers* (Eugene, OR: Harvest House Publishers, 1986) provide additional reading from a biblical perspective.

Avery Gilbert's *What the Nose Knows—The Science of Scent in Everyday Life* (New York: Crown Publishers, 2008) provides more background from the perspective of science. Also see Mandy Aftel's book *Essence and Alchemy: A Natural History of Perfume* (New York: North Point Press, 2001) and B. Gibbons article, "The Intimate Sense of Smell" (*National Geographic Society Magazine* 170:3:324-360). For a more historical overview see Diane Ackerman's book *A Natural History of the Senses* (New York: Vantage Books, 1995) and Richard L. Doty's chapter "Introduction and Historical Perspective" in *Handbook of Olfaction and Gustation* (New York: Marcel Dekker, Inc., 1995).

Internet searches can provide interesting links to information on the senses, although many sites still limit the discussion to the five common senses. A site that provides state-of-the-art findings on the human senses is www.monell.org for the Monell Chemical Senses Center in Philadelphia. The Smell and Taste Center in Philadelphia has interesting information on the senses from a medical perspective, and can be found at www.med.upenn.edu/stc. Visit the site: www.sensory-processing-disorder.com to better understand the effects of injury, disorders, or diseases on the sensory system, and their treatment. The National Institutes of Health maintain the site: www.nidcd.nih.gov/health/smelltaste.

For information on pain see "The Changing Science of Pain" by Mary Carmichael in *Newsweek* magazine (June 4, 2007; pp. 40-45). For information on pain see: www.painfoundation.org (The American Pain Foundation), www.ampainsoc.org (American Pain Society), or visit: www.headaches.org (National Headache Foundation). Visit www.essentialtremor.org for more information on body tremors (Essential Tremor Foundation).

For information on the importance of the face in relationships refer to J. Cole's book *About Face* (Cambridge, MA: The MIT Press, 1999). A facial repertoire is found at www.paulekman.com where the work of Dr. Paul Ekman can be accessed.

For background on beverages that have influenced history see T. Standage's *A History of the World in 6 Glasses* (New York: Walker and Company, 2005). For information on wine flavors consult: http://wineserver.ucdavis.edu; www.winearomawheel.com; and www.winepros.org. For a library of essential oils, the plants they come from, and odor characteristics, visit www.bojensen.net. Visit www. aftelier.com or www.essentialoils.org for information on perfume.

For Immediate Release

* * *

Healthy Life Press
David B. Biebel, Publisher
2603 Drake Drive • Orlando, FL 32810

info@healthylifepress.com
www.healthylifepress.com

Richer Descriptions
by Gary A. Burlingame

A Guide to the Human Senses
For Christian Speakers and Writers

ISBN: 978-1-9392-6732-0
Soft cover: $15.95; eBook: $9.99
6 x 9 • 238 pages

Printed book AND full-color eBook set: $22.95, only from the publisher (with free shipping for printed book) at:
www.healthylifepress.com

Printed book also available via online or other bookstores worldwide, including our primary distributor, Amazon.com.

eBooks available at: www.eChristian.com; www.Amazon.com (Kindle); and www.BN.com (Nook).

Bookseller terms available. E-mail: info@healthylifepress.com for details.

About the Book

Richer Descriptions is a unique and handy manual, covering all nine human senses in seven chapters, for Christian speakers and writers. Exercises and a speaker's checklist equip speakers to engage their audiences in a richer experience. Writing examples and a writer's guide help writers bring more life to the characters and scenes of their stories. Bible references encourage a deeper appreciation of being created by God for a sensory existence.

From the Book

Imagine going to church on a Saturday or Sunday morning. You park your car beneath a willow's shade and walk toward a stone church that proclaims that God is the rock of your life. In front, evergreen trees of various sizes and textures proclaim that Jesus is the way to eternal life. Down a path of lilies of all kinds and colors, you are reminded that your Lord cares for you more than the lilies of the field. An open door welcomes you inside where a deacon anoints your feet with spikenard, an anointing oil, because Jesus became a servant for you. Deeper inside, beneath a stone arch, another deacon sprays your outer garments with a mist of myrrh, aloes and cassia: the scent of the prophets and the priests, of which Christ is chief among them. Fragrant sandalwood, cedar, and acacia crafted pews, flooring, and altar catch the light of the morning sun streaming through an ornate stained glass window. The choir, accompanied by flute and harp, fill the sanctuary with David's Psalms, which touch on every emotion known to mankind. Out the north side windows you see a grove of apple trees and recall that you are among the people of God, the bride of Christ. Out the south-side windows you see a grove of fig trees and recall the beauty of creation, and yet Jesus died on a tree to redeem His creation. The offering plate, its cedar bottom scented with aloes, passes through your hands as you return your tithe with gladness of heart.

About the Author

Gary A. Burlingame has researched and lectured internationally on the use of the human senses to make observations on manmade and natural environments. In *Richer Descriptions*, he helps Christian speakers and writers better apply sensory imagery to their writing as well as to their speaking. Biblical references, scientific facts, and links to online resources are also provided. This is his fifth book with Healthy Life Press.

RESOURCES FROM HEALTHY LIFE PRESS

Unless otherwise noted on the site itself, shipping is free for all products purchased through www.healthylifepress.com.

NEW RELEASES – FALL 2014

Mommy, What's 'Died' Mean? - How the Butterfly Story Helped Little Dave Understand His Grandpa's Death, by Linda Swain Gill; Illustrated by David Lee Bass (a.k.a. "Little Dave") – Designed to assist Christian parents and other adults who love and care about children to talk with them about the difficult subject of death, the story traces a small child's experience following his grandpa's and shows how his mother sensitively answered his questions about death by using simple examples derived from the birth of a butterfly. Little Dave's story is colorfully illustrated and designed for a child and parent or trusted adult to read together. The story has been created especially for children from pre-kindergarten through 4th grade. Discussion questions are included for each story page to help determine how much the child understands. A simple imitation game is also included to help involve the child in the story. Several pages at the end of the book contain suggestions about how to discuss death and dying with children of various ages. (**Full-color printed book:** $14.99; PDF eBook: $9.99; both together: $19.99 – direct from publisher; printed books and eBooks available at *www.Amazon.com*; *www.BN.com*; *www.deepershopping.com*, and wherever books are sold.)

No Worries - Spiritual and Mental Health Counseling for Anxiety, by Elaine Leong Eng, MD – Offering a unique spiritual and mental health perspective on a major malady of our age, this practicing Christian psychiatrist has packed a dose of reality mixed with medicine and faith into a book aimed at informing, inspiring, and equipping those who wish to better help those who struggle with anxiety and related disorders, both inside and outside the church. As one endorser said, "I travel all over the world. I see fellow believers suffering from different forms of anxiety and worry. Dr. Eng's book gives me tools to recognize when people are suffering and how to encourage them to get the help they need." (Printed book: $19.99; PDF eBook: $9.99; both together: $24.99 – direct from publisher; printed books and eBooks available at *www.Amazon.com*; *www.BN.com*; *www.deepershopping.com*, and wherever books are sold.)

If God Is So Good, Why Do I Hurt So Bad?, by David B. Biebel, DMin – This **25th Anniversary Edition** of a best-selling classic (over 200,000 copies in print worldwide, in a dozen languages) is the book's first major revision since its initial release in 1989. This new version features additional original material related to the conundrum of suffering and faith (with principles learned along the way), and chapter ending questions for personal or group use. Endorser Sheila Walsh wrote, "I believe this is one of the most profound, empathetic and beautiful books ever written on the subject of suffering and loss. There is no attempt to quickly ease our pain but rather, with an understanding born in the crucible God uniquely designed for him, David offers a place to stand, a place to fall and a place to rise again. This book left an indelible mark on my heart over twenty years ago and now with this new release the gift is fresh and fragrant. I highly commend this to you!" (Printed book: $14.99; PDF eBook: $9.99; both together: $19.95 – direct from publisher; printed books and eBooks available at *www.Amazon.com*; *www.BN.com*; *www.deepershopping.com*, and wherever books are sold.)

Earlier Releases

We've Got Mail: The New Testament Letters in Modern English – As Relevant Today as Ever! by Rev. Warren C. Biebel, Jr. – A modern English paraphrase of the New Testament Letters, sure to inspire in readers a loving appreciation for God's Word. (Printed book: $9.95; PDF eBook: $6.95; both together: $15.00 – direct from publisher; printed books and eBooks available at *www.Amazon.com*; *www.BN.com*; *www.deepershopping.com*, and wherever books are sold.)

Hearth & Home – Recipes for Life, by Karey Swan (7th Edition) – Far more than a cookbook, this classic is a life book, with recipes for life as well as for great food. Karey describes how to buy and prepare from scratch a wide variety of tantalizing dishes, while weaving into the book's fabric the wisdom of the ages plus the recipe that she and her husband used to raise their kids. A great gift for Christmas or for a new bride. (Perfect Bound book [8 x 10, glossy cover]: $17.95; PDF eBook: $12.95; both together: $24.95 – direct from publisher; printed books and eBooks available at *www.Amazon.com*; *www.BN.com*; *www.deepershopping.com*, and wherever books are sold.)

Who Me, Pray? Prayer 101: Praying Aloud, for Beginners, by Gary A. Burlingame – Who Me, Pray? is a practical guide for prayer, based on Jesus' direction in "The Lord's Prayer," with examples provided for use in typical situations where you might be asked or expected to pray in public. (Printed book: $6.95; PDF eBook: $2.99; both together: $7.95 – direct from publisher; printed books and eBooks available at *www.Amazon.com*; *www.BN.com*; *www.deepershopping.com*, and wherever books are sold.)

My Broken Heart Sings, the poetry of Gary Burlingame – In 1987, Gary and his wife Debbie lost their son Christopher John, at only six months of age, to a chronic lung disease. This life-changing experience gave them a special heart for helping others through similar loss and pain. (Printed book: $10.95; PDF eBook: $6.95; both together: $13.95 – direct from publisher; printed books and eBooks available at *www.Amazon.com*; *www. BN.com*; *www.deepershopping.com*, and wherever books are sold.)

After Normal: One Teen's Journey Following Her Brother's Death, by Diane Aggen – Based on a journal the author kept following her younger brother's death. It offers helpful insights and understanding for teens facing a similar loss or for those who might wish to understand and help teens facing a similar loss. (Printed book: $11.95; PDF eBook: $6.95; both together: $15.00 – direct from publisher; printed books and eBooks

available at *www.Amazon.com*; *www.BN.com*; *www.deepershopping.com*, and wherever books are sold.)

In the Unlikely Event of a Water Landing – Lessons Learned from Landing in the Hudson River, by Andrew Jamison, MD – The author was flying standby on US Airways Flight 1549 toward Charlotte on January 15, 2009, from New York City, where he had been interviewing for a residency position. Little did he know that the next stop would be the Hudson River. Riveting and inspirational, this book would be especially helpful for people in need of hope and encouragement. (Printed book: $8.95; PDF eBook: $6.95; both together: $12.95 – direct from publisher; printed books and eBooks available at *www.Amazon.com*; *www.BN.com*; *www.deepershopping.com*, and wherever books are sold.)

Finding Martians in the Dark – Everything I Needed to Know About Teaching Took Me Only 30 Years to Learn, by Dan M. Biebel – Packed with wise advice based on hard experience, and laced with humor, this book is a perfect teacher's gift year-round. Susan J. Wegmann, PhD, says, "Biebel's sardonic wit is mellowed by a genuine love for kids and teaching. . . . A Whitman-like sensibility flows through his stories of teaching, learning, and life."

(Printed book: $10.95; PDF eBook: $6.95; Together: $15.00 – direct from publisher; printed books and eBooks available at *www.Amazon.com*; *www.BN.com*; *www.deepershopping.com*, and wherever books are sold.)

Because We're Family and **Because We're Friends**, by Gary A. Burlingame – Sometimes things related to faith can be hard to discuss with your family and friends. These booklets are designed to be given as gifts, to help you open the door to discussing spiritual matters with family members and friends who are open to such a conversation. (Printed book: $5.95 each; PDF eBook: $4.95 each; both together: $9.95 [printed & eBook of the same title] – direct from publisher; printed books and eBooks available at *www.Amazon.com*; *www.BN.com*; *www.deepershopping.com*, and wherever books are sold.)

**The Transforming Power of Story: How Telling Your Story Brings Hope to Others and Healing to Yourself,** by Elaine Leong Eng, MD, and David B. Biebel, DMin – This book demonstrates, through multiple true life stories, how sharing one's story, especially in a group setting, can bring hope to listeners and healing to the one who shares. Individuals facing difficulties will find this book greatly encouraging. (Printed book: $14.99; PDF eBook: $9.99; both together: $19.99 – direct from publisher; printed books and eBooks available at *www.Amazon.com*; *www.BN.com*; *www.deepershopping.com*, and wherever books are sold.)

You Deserved a Better Father: Good Parenting Takes a Plan, by Robb Brandt, MD – About parenting by intention, and other lessons the author learned through the loss of his firstborn son. It is especially for parents who believe that bits and pieces of leftover time will be enough for their own children. (Printed book: $12.95 each; PDF eBook: $6.95; both together: $17.95 – direct from publisher; printed books and eBooks available at *www.Amazon.com*; *www.BN.com*; *www.deepershopping.com*, and wherever books are sold.)

**Jonathan, You Left Too Soon**, by David B. Biebel, DMin – One pastor's journey through the loss of his son, into the darkness of depression, and back into the light of joy again, emerging with a renewed sense of mission. (Printed book: $12.95; PDF eBook: $5.99; both together: $15.00 – direct from publisher; printed books and eBooks available at *www.Amazon.com*; *www.BN.com*; *www.deepershopping.com*, and wherever books are sold.)

Unless otherwise noted on the site itself, shipping is free for all products purchased through <u>*www.healthylifepress.com*</u>*.*

The Spiritual Fitness Checkup for the 50-Something Woman, by Sharon V. King, PhD – Following the stages of a routine medical exam, the author describes ten spiritual fitness "checkups" midlife women can conduct to assess their spiritual health and tone up their relationship with God. Each checkup consists of the author's personal reflections, a Scripture reference for meditation, and a "Spiritual Pulse Check," with exercises readers can use for personal application. (Printed book: $8.95; PDF eBook: $6.95; both together: $12.95 – direct from publisher; printed books and eBooks available at *www.Amazon.com*; *www.BN.com*; *www.deepershopping.com*, and wherever books are sold.)

The Other Side of Life – Over 60? God Still Has a Plan for You, by Rev. Warren C. Biebel, Jr. – Drawing on biblical examples and his 60-plus years of pastoral experience, Rev. Biebel helps older (and younger) adults understand God's view of aging and the rich life available to everyone who seeks a deeper relationship with God as they age. Rev. Biebel explains how to: Identify God's ongoing plan for your life; Rely on faith to manage the anxieties of aging;  Form positive, supportive relationships; Cultivate patience; Cope with new technologies; Develop spiritual integrity; Understand the effects of dementia; Develop a Christ-centered perspective of aging. (Printed book: $10.95; PDF eBook: $6.95; both together: $15.00 – direct from publisher; printed books and eBooks available at *www.Amazon.com*; *www.BN.com*; *www.deepershopping.com*, and wherever books are sold.)

My Faith, My Poetry, by Gary A. Burlingame – This unique book of Christian poetry is actually two in one. The first collection of poems, A Day in the Life, explores a working parent's daily journey of faith. The reader is carried from morning to bedtime, from "In the Details," to "I Forgot to Pray," back to "Home Base," and finally to "Eternal Love Divine." The second collection of poems, Come Running, is wonder, joy, and faith wrapped up in words that encourage and inspire the mind and the heart. (Printed book: $10.95; PDF eBook: $6.95; both together: $13.95 – direct from publisher; printed books and eBooks available at *www.Amazon.com*; *www.BN.com*; *www.deepershopping.com*, and wherever books are sold.)

On Eagles' Wings, by Sara Eggleston – One woman's life journey from idyllic through chaotic to joy, carried all the way by the One who has promised to never leave us nor forsake us. Remarkable, poignant, moving, and inspiring, this autobiographical account will help many who are facing difficulties that seem too great to overcome or even bear at all. It is proof that Isaiah 40:31 is as true today as when it was penned, "But they that wait upon the LORD shall renew their strength; they shall mount up with wings as eagles; they shall run, and not be weary; and they shall walk, and not faint." (Printed book: $14.95; PDF eBook: $8.95; both together: $22.95 – direct from publisher; printed books and eBooks available at *www.Amazon.com*; *www.BN.com*; *www.deepershopping.com*, and wherever books are sold.)

Richer Descriptions, by Gary A. Burlingame – A unique and handy manual, covering all nine human senses in seven chapters, for Christian speakers and writers. Exercises and a speaker's checklist equip speakers to engage their audiences in a richer experience. Writing examples and a writer's guide help writers bring more life to the characters and scenes of their stories. Bible references encourage a deeper appreciation of being created by God for a sensory existence. (Printed book: $15.95; PDF eBook: $8.95; both together: $22.95 – direct from publisher; printed books and eBooks available at *www.Amazon.com*; *www.BN.com*; *www.deepershopping.com*, and wherever books are sold.)

Treasuring Grace, by Rob Plumley and Tracy Roberts – This novel was inspired by a dream. Liz Swanson's life isn't quite what she'd imagined, but she considers herself lucky. She has a good husband, beautiful children, and fulfillment outside of her home through volunteer work. On some days she doesn't even notice the dull ache in her heart. While she's preparing for their summer kickoff at Lake George, the ache disappears and her sudden happiness is mistaken for anticipation of their weekend. However, as the family heads north, there are clouds on the horizon that have nothing to do with the weather. Only Liz's daughter, who's found some of her mother's hidden journals, has any idea what's wrong. But by the end of the weekend, there will be no escaping the truth or its painful buried secrets.

(Printed: $12.95; PDF eBook: $7.95; both together: $19.95 – direct from publisher; printed books and eBooks available at *www.Amazon.com*; *www.BN.com*; *www.deepershopping.com*, and wherever books are sold.)

From Orphan to Physician – The Winding Path, by Chun-Wai Chan, MD – From the foreword: "In this book, Dr. Chan describes how his family escaped to Hong Kong, how they survived in utter poverty, and how he went from being an orphan to graduating from Harvard Medical School and becoming a cardiologist. The writing is fluent, easy to read and understand. The sequence of events is realistic, emotionally moving, spiritually touching, heartwarming, and thought provoking. The book illustrates . . . how one must have faith in order to walk through life's winding path." (Printed book: $14.95; PDF eBook: $8.95; both together: $22.95 – direct from publisher; printed books and eBooks available at *www.Amazon.com*; *www.BN.com*; *www.deepershopping.com*, and wherever books are sold.)

12 Parables, by Wayne Faust – Timeless Christian stories about doubt, fear, change, grief, and more. Using tight, entertaining prose, professional musician and comedy performer Wayne Faust manages to deal with difficult concepts in a simple, straightforward way. These are stories you can read aloud over and over—to your spouse, your family, or in a group setting. Packed with emotion and just enough mystery to keep you wondering, while  providing lots of points to ponder and discuss when you're through, these stories relate the gospel in the tradition of the greatest speaker of parables the world has ever known, who appears in them often. (Printed book: $14.95; PDF eBook: $8.95; both together: $22.95 – direct from publisher; printed books and eBooks available at *www.Amazon.com*; *www.BN.com*; *www.deepershopping.com*, and wherever books are sold.)

The Answer is Always "Jesus," by Aram Haroutunian, who gave children's sermons for 15 years at a large church in Golden, Colorado—well over 500 in all. This book contains 74 of his most unforgettable presentations—due to the children's responses. Pastors, homeschoolers, parents who often lead family devotions, or other storytellers will find these stories, along with comments about props and how to prepare and present them, an invaluable asset in reconnecting with the simplest, most profound truths of Scripture, and then to envision how best to communicate these so even a child can understand them. (Printed book: $12.95; PDF eBook: $8.95; both together: $19.95 – direct from publisher; printed books and eBooks available at *www.Amazon.com*; *www.BN.com*; *www.deepershopping.com*, and wherever books are sold.)

Handbook of Faith, by Rev. Warren C. Biebel, Jr. – The New York Times World 2011 Almanac claimed that there are 2 billion, 200 thousand Christians in the world, with "Christians" being defined as "followers of Christ." The original 12 followers of Christ changed the world; indeed, they changed the history of the world. So this author, a pastor with over 60 years' experience, poses and answers this logical question: "If there are so many 'Christians' on this planet, why are they so relatively ineffective in serving the One they claim to follow?" Answer: Because, unlike Him, they do not know and trust the Scriptures, implicitly. This little volume will help you do that. (Printed book: $8.95; PDF eBook: $6.95; both together: $13.95 – direct from publisher; printed books and eBooks available at *www.Amazon.com*; *www.BN.com*; *www.deepershopping.com*, and wherever books are sold.)

Pieces of My Heart, by David L. Wood – Eighty-two lessons from normal everyday life. David's hope is that these stories will spark thoughts about God's constant involvement and intervention in our lives and stir a sense of how much He cares about every detail that is important to us. The piece missing represents his son, Daniel, who died in a fire shortly before his first birthday.  (Printed book: $16.95; PDF eBook: $8.95; both together: $24.95 – direct from publisher; printed books and eBooks available at *www.Amazon.com*; *www.BN.com*; *www.deepershopping.com*, and wherever books are sold.)

Unless otherwise noted on the site itself, shipping is free for all products purchased through <u>www.healthylifepress.com</u>.

**Dream House**, by Justa Carpenter – Written by a New England builder of several hundred homes, the idea for this book came to him one day as he was driving that came to him one day as was driving from one job site to another. He pulled over and recorded it so he would remember it, and now you will remember it, too, if you believe, as he does, that ". . . He who has begun a good work in you will complete it until the day of Jesus Christ." (Printed book: $10.95; PDF eBook: $6.95; both together: $13.95 – direct from publisher; printed books and eBooks available at *www.Amazon.com*; *www.BN.com*; *www.deepershopping.com*, and wherever books are sold.)

A Simply Homemade Clean, by homesteader Lisa Barthuly – "Somewhere along the path, it seems we've lost our gumption, the desire to make things ourselves," says the author. "Gone are the days of 'do it yourself.' Really . . . why bother? There are a slew of retailers just waiting for us with anything and everything we could need; packaged up all pretty, with no thought or effort required. It is the manifestation of 'progress' . . . right?" I don't buy  that!" Instead, Lisa describes how to make safe and effective cleansers for home, laundry, and body right in your own home. This saves money and avoids exposure to harmful chemicals often found in commercially produced cleansers. (**Full-color** printed book: $16.99; PDF eBook: $6.95; both together: $22.95 – direct from publisher; printed books and eBooks available at *www.Amazon.com*; *www.BN.com*; *www.deepershopping.com*, and wherever books are sold.)

**The Secret of Singing Springs**, by Monte Swan – One Colorado family's treasure-hunting adventure along the trail of Jesse James. The Secret of Singing Springs is written to capture for children and their parents the spirit of the hunt—the hunt for treasure as in God's Truth, which is the objective of walking the Way of Wisdom that is described in Proverbs. (Printed book: $12.95, PDF eBook: $9.99; both together: $19.99 – direct from publisher; printed books and eBooks available at *www.Amazon.com*; *www.BN.com*; *www.deepershopping.com*, and wherever books are sold.)

God Loves You Circle, by Michelle Johnson – Daily inspiration for your deeper walk with Christ. This collection of short stories of Christian living will make you laugh, make you cry, but most of all make you contemplate—the meaning and value of walking with the Master moment-by-moment, day-by-day. (**Full-color** printed book: $17.95; PDF eBook: $9.99; both together: $22.99 – direct from publisher; printed books and eBooks available at *www.Amazon.com*; *www.BN.com*; *www.deepershopping.com*, and wherever books are sold.)

Our God-Given Senses, by Gary A. Burlingame – Did you know humans have NINE senses? The Bible draws on these senses to reveal spiritual truth. We are to taste and see that the Lord is a good. We are to carry the fragrance of Christ. Our faith is produced upon hearing. Jesus asked Thomas to touch him. God created us for a sensory experience and that is what you will find in this book. (Printed book: $12.99; PDF eBook: $9.99; both together: $19.99 – direct from publisher; printed books and eBooks available at *www.Amazon.com*; *www.BN.com*; *www.deepershopping.com*, and wherever books are sold.)

Vows, a Romantic novel by F. F. Whitestone – When the police cruiser pulled up to the curb outside, Faith Framingham's heart skipped a beat, for she could see that Chuck, who should have been driving, was not in the vehicle. Chuck's partner, Sandy, stepped out slowly. Sandy's pursed lips and ashen face spoke volumes. Faith waited by the front door, her hands clasped tightly, to counter the fact that her mind was already reeling. "Love never fails." A compelling story. (Printed book: $12.99; PDF eBook: $9.99; both together, $19.99 – direct from publisher; printed books and eBooks available at *www.Amazon.com*; *www.BN.com*; *www.deepershopping.com*, and wherever books are sold.)

Unless otherwise noted on the site itself, shipping is free for all products purchased through www.healthylifepress.com.

Worth the Cost?, by Jack Tsai, MD – The author was happily on his way to obtaining the American Dream until he decided to take seriously Jesus' command, "Come, follow me." Join him as he explores the cost of medical education and Christian discipleship. Planning to serve God in your future vocation? Take care that your desires do not get side-tracked by the false promises of this world. What you should be doing now so when you are done with your training you will still want to serve God. (Printed book: $12.99, PDF eBook: $9.99; both together: $19.99 – direct from publisher; printed books and eBooks available at *www.Amazon.com*; *www.BN.com*; *www.deepershopping.com*, and wherever books are sold.)

Nature: God's Second Book – An Essential Link to Restoring Your Personal Health and Wellness: Body, Mind, and Spirit, by Elvy P. Rolle – An inspirational book that looks at nature across the seasons of nature and of life. It uses the biblical Emmaus Journey as an analogy for life's journey, and offers ideas for using nature appreciation and exploration to reduce life's stresses. The  author shares her personal story of how she came to grips with this concept after three trips to the emergency room. (**Full-color** printed book: $12.99; PDF eBook $8.99; both together: $16.99 – direct from publisher; printed books and eBooks available at *www.Amazon.com*; *www.BN.com*; *www.deepershopping.com*, and wherever books are sold.)

He Waited, by LaDonna Cooper – Inspires readers to wait upon the Lord for His best for them; stresses the importance of putting God's purpose above one's own; emphasizes that God's love is unconditional; demonstrates the wisdom of waiting, through a combination of positive insights, encouragement, biblical examples and principles. Decorated with original poetry by the author. For singles and others who are waiting. Distributed primarily through *www.Amazon.com*. (Printed book: $10.99; PDF eBook: $9.99; both together: $15.99 – direct from publisher; printed books and eBooks available at *www.Amazon.com*; *www.BN.com*; *www.deepershopping.com*, and wherever books are sold.)

Seasonal

 **The Big Black Book – What the Christmas Tree Saw**, by Rev. Warren C. Biebel, Jr. – An original Christmas story, from the perspective of the Christmas tree. This little book is especially suitable for parents to read to their children at Christmas time or all year-round. (**Full-color** printed book: $9.95; PDF eBook: $4.95; both together: $12.95 – direct from publisher; printed books and eBooks available at *www.Amazon.com*; *www.BN.com*; *www.deepershopping.com*, and wherever books are sold.)

About Healthy Life Press

Healthy Life Press was founded with a primary goal of helping previously unpublished authors to get their works to market, and to reissue worthy, previously published works that were no longer available. Our mission is to help people toward optimal vitality by providing resources promoting physical, emotional, spiritual, and relational health as viewed from a Christian perspective. We see health as a verb, and achieving optimal health as a process—a crucial process for followers of Christ if we are to love the Lord with all our heart, soul, mind, AND strength, and our neighbors as ourselves—for as long as He leaves us here. We are a collaborative and cooperative small Christian publisher. We share costs/we share proceeds.

For information about publishing with us, e-mail: <u>healthylifepress@aol.com</u>.

www.ingramcontent.com/pod-product-compliance
Lightning Source LLC
Chambersburg PA
CBHW052106070526
44584CB00017B/2364